POEMS FROM MY HEART AND SOUL

Melvin Avery Edwards

Wendy,
To a good friend who believed in me and my book. May God bless you and your family always
Melvin Avery Edwards
3/8/2010

AuthorHouse™
1663 Liberty Drive
Bloomington, IN 47403
www.authorhouse.com
Phone: 1-800-839-8640

© *2010 Melvin Avery Edwards. All rights reserved.*

No part of this book may be reproduced, stored in a retrieval system, or transmitted by any means without the written permission of the author.

First published by AuthorHouse 2/16/2010

ISBN: 978-1-4490-2487-1 (e)
ISBN: 978-1-4490-2485-7 (sc)
ISBN: 978-1-4490-2486-4 (hc)

Library of Congress Control Number: 2010901292

Printed in the United States of America
Bloomington, Indiana

This book is printed on acid-free paper.

Table of Contents

Forward vii

Acknowledgments ix

Friends To The End 1

Thoughts From A Black Man 11

Love 27

Dedicated To My Sister Madeline Patricia Edwards 45

For All The Women Who Make Life Great 53

Christmas...63

Different Thoughts About Life On This Earth.............................73

Conclusion 89

FORWARD

For a number of years I have been writing poems for myself and others in good times, bad times, or indifferent times in my life. It has seemed to relieve my stress in times of pain and happiness. Some of my poems have brought comfort to others in their times of need. I did not want everyone to read my poems and the feelings that were on display in the poems I wrote and I did not want others to be judgmental on what I had written and how I perceive life on this earth.

I have only shared my poems with close friends and family (as you know some people are not overly thrilled when asked to read anyone's poetry). Of cause not everyone will like what I had written, but for the most part, people that have read them seemed to enjoy the poems. My friends in the past several years have asked me why not share your poetry and let others enjoy your works as we have?

Thus, I decided to write this book of poetry to share with the world. I did not write this book to become world famous or to make a lot of money. I wrote this book with hopes that as others read the poems it will inspire them to write poems from their hearts in times of their lives when they are happy, sad or depressed. I hope that some of my poems will cause people to look at life from a different point of view.

I have found that my poems are a good place to put down what I am feeling at different times of my life. Sometimes when I go back and read what I have written in the past I am shocked that those thoughts came from me and that GOD has given me this talent.

ACKNOWLEDGMENTS

I would like to thank all my friends and relatives who encouraged me when I was not making anything of my life and seemed to be headed down river fast without a lifeboat. I would also like to thank them for believing in me even when I did not believe in myself.

I would like to thank several people from Saint Louis University who were instrumental in helping with this project and the completion of this book:

Avis Myers PH. D
Jiao (Maggie) Ma PH. D
Kay Bopp (Parks College)

Most of all I would like to thank my mother (Jessie M. Johnson) who never gave up hope that I would someday be successful in this life and always encouraged me even when I was trying to destroy myself in the way I was living my life. Thanks **MAMA** I will always love you, this book is for you. May GOD keep you here on this earth for many more years to come!

Melvin Avery Edwards

Poems are messages from the writer that give the reader insight into the inner thoughts of the writer's mind. Poems are meant to inspire whoever is reading them to write their thoughts down on a page and hopefully enrich their lives as my poems have enriched mine.

FRIENDS TO THE END

A friend is someone you can trust with your life and know that they will not let you down when you need them the most. You hope they will be around on this earth for as long as you are.

FRIENDS NEVER END

When I first saw you, you were just another face in the crowd
Someone not to be remembered right away
Then I met you and begin to talk with you
It was like when you turn on the light in the room
Suddenly you can see the whole room so it was with you
I began to see the real person you are
Not just someone to be lusted after
But someone real, to love, to hold, to be friends with
Someone who would make a man happy to be alive
Happy that he has you in his life
Happy to share whatever he has with you
To give you everything your heart desires
To walk in the park, holding hands
Not caring about what's going on in this world
Knowing that as long as he has you by his side he can face anything
In this world and win
But I realize that this can never be
For you belong to another

We are like two ships passing in the night, never to touch
I am in one ship, wishing to reach you, to touch you, to share you
To love you as a man is supposed to love a woman
But you're already sharing your ship with another, happy with life
For even though I cannot have you the way I want
Friendship is a life of beauty also
For a friend can be someone to share life with
Someone to hold you when you are down
Someone to listen when you need to talk
To be there when others have let you down
For anyone can make love to another, but all cannot be friends

So my friend, turn not your back on me
Never let anything interrupt our friendships
And I will be there when you need me

And you when I need you
To fight the battles of this world
For a friend is like a life raft on a ship
Like a glass of water to a thirsty man
So let not our friendship end
Because of the stupid people of this world
For even though I cannot have you for my own
I can always have you as a friend
And you also will have a friend
Till this world is no longer here

A FRIEND THAT SAVES

He is the one I look up to when I'm feeling down
He is the only one that can always take away my frown
He is the one who is always there when I am feeling blue
He is the one who will always be there telling me the true
He's there no matter what the time of day or night
He's holding me when I am full of fright on a sleepless night
He is my friend, He is my friend, and Jesus will have mercy on me
He is the one who makes my world, Jesus have mercy on me

He's there when people have gone away and left you all alone
He is the one I can depend on when all other hope is gone
He is the one who is there when family and friends turn their back on you
He is the one who will always be there to help you make it through this life
He is there when you seem to be going downhill and will love you no matter what you do
He is the one that will pull you through and keep you from feeling blue
He is my friend, He is my friend, and Jesus will have mercy on me
He is the one who makes my world, Jesus have mercy on me

He is my King, Life and Friend when everyone around is wearing a frown
He will one day lead me to Heaven where I will turn in my frown for a crown
He will fill my soul with joy and happiness for the rest of my days on earth
He will be there when death has taken me away from this place
He will finally let me see Him face to face because of His saving grace
He will know that I have always wanted His saving grace while on this earth
He is my friend, He is my friend, and Jesus will have mercy on me
He is the one who makes my world, Jesus have mercy on me

FRIEND

A friend is someone who inspires you and helps you to become a better person
Someone who is there when you are down and there when things are good
Someone who doesn't judge you or put you down when you make a mistake
Someone who believes in you even when you don't believe in yourself
Someone who is willing to help you in times of need and not say you own them for life
Someone who doesn't have to put you down to feel good about themselves
Someone who is patient with you, even when you make the same mistakes over and over again
Someone who is willing to guide you in the right direction and teach you what they know
Someone whose dream for you is to be as successful as you can be and more

Yes, you are the kind of friend who makes people want to be a success
You make people what to be better human beings and help others
You inspire people to be better than they thought they were able to be
Your friendship shows people what God wants us to be towards each other
Your teachings make people want to be all that they can be in this life
You help to make the world a better place each day that you are in it
You inspire me to want to be the type of friend you are to me to everyone I come in contact with
For you live God's words, do unto others as you would have them do unto you
And as long as God grants me breath in my body I will always count you as my friend

THAT SPECIAL LADY

When I was just a little boy, I didn't know what to do
But I always had this lady, who helped make my dreams come true
And without this special lady, those little dreams would have been blue
That's why I will always call her when I do not know what to do in this life
That's why I will call her mama until the day I die and leave this earth to see the man upstairs

And as I became older and looked back on my life, mama always knew what was best
This lady was special in all the things she's done for me while I was a child
She taught me how to live, how to save and to forgive others when they treated me wrong
But most of all she taught me how to make this world a better place to live
That's why I will call her mama until the day I die and leave this earth to see the man upstairs

And now that I am grown I realize that she has always been my best friend
Remember all those little things she used to do that no one seems to see or care about
But I will have her memories for all the years of my life while on this earth
And all those little things she did helping me to see the reality of life
That's why I will call her mama until the day I die and leave this earth to see the man upstairs

And now that she is old it's my turn to do all these things she did for me
To make her life much easier and help her with everything she needs to do

Now I know within my heart I will never be able to do all those things she did for me
I will give my best friend all the love she gave to me all my years in this life and not let her down
That's why I will call her mama until the day I die and leave this earth to see the man upstairs

A FRIEND SHINES AT CHRISTMAS

Throughout the year you can always depend on a good friend in everyway
No matter if the chips are down, your friend will never let you stray
They are always there when life seems to pull you down
Letting you know whatever you do that Christ will help remove that frown
They let you know throughout the year that Christ is always there
And that no matter what else happens Christ will always treat you fair

Your friend is not like others whose light shine a dreary gray
Your friend's light is always bright to help you find your way
A friend does not always want something in return for what they do
They only want the best for you to keep you from feeling blue
They only want you to have the best and find the road that is right
For only through this road will you find the light of Christ

However when you are depressed, a friend's light shines a special way
And helps you always find the path that leads to back towards Christ's way
Your friend let's you know they are there whenever you need someone
And that no matter what time of day or night your friendship is always number one
Be thankful if you have a friend who will always be there to help guide your way
For I am sure that Christ will bless you both as you as past along His way

THOUGHTS FROM A BLACK MAN

Being black in America means waking up knowing that you will always be different from everyone else, no matter where you go or what you become in this life. However, you should not hold hate in your heart for those that treat you this way, for they are the ones that need understanding and love the most.

A BLACK MAN'S FATE

To be born a black man is like being born to condemnation in Hell
For this man most always prove himself in every walk he takes in life
He is forever looked upon as someone to be feared and despised
Whenever he walks down the street, people are always thinking that he will do them harm
Thinking that he is a criminal, even when he has done nothing wrong
Thinking that this black man is the cause of all the crime in this society
Thinking that he is nothing more than a savage waiting to strike his next victim
Always thinking that he should be in jail so that their streets will be safe again
And that people can rest easy in their beds at night once he is locked away

To be born a black man is like being born to a condemnation in Hell
For when the police have anything to do with him, there is no respect
There is only the belief that he is guilty of a crime, and they most lock him up
There is no treatment of him as a human being, only that of a mad dog on the loose
Thus, it is all right to beat him and chain him up like a dog
All right to lie upon him to keep him in jail far away from decent human beings
All right for a society to spit upon him, like he is the scum of the earth
To make him feel as if he should never have been born on this planet
To make him feel that his life is useless, and that even if he succeeds he still has failed

To be born a black man is like being born to a condemnation in Hell
Even among his own people he forever must defend his manhood
To always feel that he has to be able to prove to other black men that he is a man

Always battling with one another, killing one another, lying upon one another
Always believing that he cannot trust anyone, not even his woman, for she has turned on him
Forever making him feel that no matter what he does it's not good enough
For to trust someone might mean to spent all your time in jail, or death itself
To wake up to know that no matter what you do, you most do it alone
For there is no trust, no love, even in your own neighborhood

To be born a black man is like being born to a condemnation in Hell
You go through your whole life being confused, abused, and misused
Forever knowing that no matter what path you take there is no respect for you
No matter how much money you have, you are still looked upon as just another nigger
With a society waiting for you to make a mistake, so that they can put you in jail for life
And the police willing to lock you up and lie about you just because you happen to be a black man
But you must go on, because if you stop you might as well be put to death
No matter if you have to fight the whole world, you must let people know that you are someone
Someone who lives, breaths, and has emotions just like anyone else
Someone who wants the respect of others, just as they want you to respect them

ONE-DAY PEACE

One day people will be able to sit down and talk to each other
without fear of what's going to happen afterwards
Men will be able to talk of peace without the threat of violence
All colors will come together and become one
People will stop killing each other for no reason
Neighbors will be neighbors again
Doors will not have to be locked, for everyone will look out for each another
Love will be spread like wild fire, from one heart to another
God will be praised on every corner and in every house
For surely if we are to have peace with each other God will have to be somewhere around
Not just when we need each other; but in our hearts at all times
For the key to any happiness is for God to have the front seat, and for us to ride and listen.
For if you are always talking you will miss what God has to say
One day we will all be free with happiness in God's house
Don't be a lost soul falling into darkness
Come to the light of the Lord

SILENCE

Oh God can you hear the crying of this black child's heart as he sits along in the dark?
Can you hear him asking for your help and mercy as his father beats him every day of his life?
Can you hear him asking you to talk with him to let him know you are real in his time of sorry and pain?
Can you hear him calling your name late into the night when he is full of fright?
Can you hear the crying of his sisters and brothers who are hungry waiting for dad to come home?
Can you feel their hungry pains when they have not eaten food for days and they do not understand?
Can you hear them start to forsake God's love when they begin to believe it's not real?
Can you hear them say we are all along for they do not hear God's voice?
Silence! Silence! Silence!

Can you hear when men are raping him and tearing him all apart late into the night?
Can you hear your child asking you to save him from this as they abuse this child for years?
Can you see that his heart is beginning to see nothing but hate as he faints from all the pain?
Can you see this child run away and ask the police for help and relieve him from his pain?
Can you see the police tell him to go back home for you get no help tonight?
Can you feel that he has turned away and will not ask for your help for the rest of life on earth?
Can you feel that he cannot feel love in his heart again for he does not believe he has a friend?
Can you see that he thinks that he is all along and will not believe that God can stop the pain?
Silence! Silence! Silence!

Can you see that this black man has grown-up and hates all of mankind as well as God for his pain?
Can you see that he knows nothing but misery and knows not love for self or God?
Can you hear his heart crying inside for he knows not how to love himself or to rid his pain?
Can you hear his voice deep inside him crying out your name and asking for your help?
Can you not speak to this heart who wants so hard to believe that God is real this in this life?
Oh God help me this night a black man says and show me that the love you said you had for me?
Can you not see his heart is cold and in much need of God's everlasting love on this night?
Silence! Silence! Silence! Oh! Dam this awful silence that will never save my life!

USING WHAT YOU HAVE

Many things in life do not change, God knows if they only would
It would make life that much simpler so that you could do only what's right
You would know which direction to take when things are going down
The way to change it is not life itself but to change the way you think
Don't always look for the easy way out because there really isn't one
The short cuts you thought were there are but images of fantasyland
The pot at the end of the rainbow or the horse shoe that brings good luck is nothing but a change of mind because you are your only luck

Life is a game that must be played with the rules that are already there
You can't create your own rules and expect to win
You must remember that all you have tried has been tried time and time again
For many people such as you have been looking for that gold at the rainbow's end
So take the cards you have and play those cards and you will have nothing to regret
You will know in the end that you have tried with all your will and might
So if things get bad don't look around for the easy way out
Just play by the rules and in the end you will win with plenty of time to share

EVERLASTING PAIN ON EARTH

Used to love to go to my grandmother's house in Mississippi
Plenty of fun, lots to eat (cat fish, hush puppies), easy living, lots of sharing
Listening to my grandfather talk about times when he grew in the 30's and 40's
Wild times, where you had to be careful about what you said to the white man
Fun time for blacks who had their own little clubs to go to after work
Let off steam, lots of fighting, even back then
Looking for a woman was not hard; blacks more together back then

Folks all mixed up and confused my grandfather said
Really didn't know who they were, couldn't be white, couldn't be African, didn't have any roots
My grandfather told me, just like leaves blowing in the wind never able to settle anywhere
Took out anger on each other, my grandfather said
Just like now, afraid of the white man, had to go by his rules
Even if it meant going against your own family
Tried to stay together with family my grandfather said

No one knew what to say or do back then to stay ahead of the game
Had no roots to relate to, beaten out of us long ago, my grandfather said
White man wanted us to be just like them and follow the white man's rules
Even when we did we were still not wanted in white man's neighborhoods
They still had fun growing up down in Mississippi, playing cards and other games after work
Nothing else to do to relieve the pain of not having a country to be welcome in
A country that you could relate to not always searching for hope in this land my grandfather said

We never understood what we were looking for, always empty inside
Like something is missing; couldn't relate to the white man's history
Had to learn this history anyway, my grandfather said
Never was able to believe anything that was said to me by the white man
He was always changing the rules on you if he thought you were getting too far ahead
Tried to go along with the program, but we were always lost
As to what was right and what was wrong, what was law and what that law meant
Whites were always changing laws my grandfather said
No matter what blacks did they were always somehow breaking the laws of the land

If my grandfather was still alive he would know that nothing has changed
All the same, still lost, no country, no hope, murdering each other even faster now
All we want is to be treated the same as everyone else
No one listens; people do not care about our pains on this earth
Listening to my grandfather's stories of growing up was fun
Too bad we can't go back home, have a place where we belong

LIFE AND DRINKING

Life is a jungle, you fight so hard to survive and win,
Only to lose it in one quick moment, when you begin a life of drinking
People are not born to drink, but they learn how to drink on their own
It's like taking your life in your own hands and slowly killing yourself
It doesn't make you feel good very long, but the things it has you doing can last a lifetime
It turns friends into enemies and love into hatred, makes you think you're doing right when you know you are wrong

Drinking is no excuse for lying and cheating because it catches up with you in the end
I've been down that road where there is no end and you lose all your friends
It's like taking giant steps in life to find you're only coming back where you started from
It has turned completely around, sometimes making you feel like a clown
It's no fun seeing a man who's drinking most of his life away
For it means he is running out of time to have a chance for happiness in the end

He wants to stop, but he doesn't know how
All he knows is that bottle is making him run
Running to a darkness, a darkness greater than light
Makes you wonder how he can ever stand the sight
Friends who are gone, and the family doesn't care
So there you are all alone; you sit in the darkness crying for yourself
Wondering how and why you are always wearing a frown

Your mind is a fog from that bottle you hold calling it your friend
So how can you think of anything in life when all your dreams are dimmed by rain?

If you put down that bottle and see the light, there is no more crying in the darkness of the night
Without the drinking you can deal with anything in this life
You will be surprised by the people who care and are waiting for you to change
You'll make new friends who will always want you around
You'll feel on top of the world and Jesus will be in your world

Someday you'll finally realize that drinking will keep at the bottom of the world
And the only way to make your dreams come true is to put that bottle down!
Being sober is fun, and sometimes life can be fair if you face it with a sober breath
So don't hide behind that bottle of pain because it can only bring your life full of rain
With the help of God, yourself, and friends you can hang in there for that beautiful end
For God will always be there when you need a friend and never let you down

WHAT DOES GOD DO?

God promises you life after dead, but is this really true?
No one has come back from the dead to say this is so
God does not send money down from Heaven to help the sick,
The poor, the hungry, and those who need a place to stay
God promises spiritual relieve on this earth
But where is god when you have no place to stay?
Ministers tell you to have patience and God will reward you, but most don't give you anything but prayers
Ministries say pray to God and He will give you your heart's desire, but many have died, and will die with no answer to their prayers
What does God do?

Why does God show His Light only to certain people on this earth?
Would He not better serve to show His light to everyone to believe?
Ministries say God gives you free will, but what good is free will when you are on the bottom of society
What good is free will when God says that if you don't do things His way you will be sent to Hell after you die?
God says the meek shall inherit the earth, but that is not till the end of the world, what good is it then
Different religious groups say they are the only light to the promise land
How are a man to know, what is a lie and what is the truth?
What does God do?

God made women for men, but if man loves more than one woman God says He will go to hell
Solomon and David both have more than one woman, and they were blessed by God
God says that when man is born he will be a sinner for all of his days on earth
When man sins while he is on this earth God says he will be punished for his sins, and after man dies he will go to hell, is this not double punishment

God's own word tells us that most of mankind will go to Hell
 So why does mankind go around trying to be prefect when it is a hopeless situation in the end
God says He will bless you if you serve Him while you are on this earth, so why does the good suffer the most?
God says He sees and hears everything, so why did He allow the Serpent to tempt Eve when He knew that Eve would fail?
Why did God punish all of mankind forever for this mistake on earth when He knew man would not win?
What does God do?

God lets human beings to be born on this earth to struggle and suffer while they are here, but then after all the suffering on this earth they die
For being born into a situation they did not create, and did not have anything to do with
Is this the work of a true and loving God?
If prayers are so powerful why do so many receive an answer from God of no?
Why does God allow some people to be born to suffer, while others are born to have the good life before they die?
Do not the rich and the powerful give God to the poor so that they will not rise up to take what the riches have?
If God is so powerful why does He not end this uncaring planet with all these uncaring people, to end all our suffering?
For surely a God so powerful, caring, and loving would not let this kind of suffering to go on, and on, and on
What does God do?

PRAYING

I pray and I pray to hear the call of God in my life
But most of the time I hear silence on the other end
A silence that means that I will not hear the call of God that day
It means that what I have prayed for is not for me from God above
It means that I will need to work harder in order to make it in this life
And I wonder if God is still there for me and still my friend?
Does He hear the praying everyday or is He to busy answer each and every one

I pray and I pray to hear the call of God in my life
I wonder if sometimes I have dialed up a wrong number to this place in the sky
And that God only answers His chosen few who have a special place up there
For it seems to me that only the rich can get through to God and get an answer
While those suffering on this earth cannot get through to God on the other end
And go on suffering on this earth until the day they die on this earth
Never knowing what they needed to do to hear the call of God before they left

I pray and I pray to hear the call of God in my life
Sometimes when it is too late and people have suffered while they wait
The world gets worse and worse as God sits upon His throng in the sky
The cries grow louder and louder from the children who are being hurt
As they wait for God to delivery they from their misery on earth
When that day comes when God returns to this earth to save us
Will people be happy to hear that call or will they run from this God from above?

LOVE

Love can leave you feeling good about yourself or make you feel that your life has no meaning at any given time. However, a life without love is a life that has not been lived to its fullest.

A PASSING FANTASY

When I first saw you there I didn't know what to say
Then you came over to and said, "Baby that's okay"
You have the looks of an angel sweetest looks I ever did see
And the smile of a baby that could only be for me

And maybe someday you will be able to see
How I really love you, and this feeling inside of me
And as I sit here looking, I have so much to say
And baby you're the only one that I could ever want stay

And as the days go by I have this passing fear
That if I wait much longer you will be gone away from here
So if things don't all work out at least I'll always know
I came close to that true love that I really wanted to know

So as you go away from me I feel that little pain
But I still have those memories of those times there was no rain
And as you go on your way I hope you will find
The love that you are seeking and all those happy times

THE THINGS YOU DO

I love the way you talk to me
The way you hold your head and smile
I love the way you hold my hand
When you've been gone for a little while
But baby most of all
I just love you plain and true
Cause baby when I'm with you
I know my days will not be blue

I love the way you look at me
When you have something to say
The way you hold me in your arms
And say baby you're okay
The smile when you are happy
The look when you sad
But most of all baby
You just make me feel good when I am feeling blue

I love the way you walk with me
The way you hold your head up high
The way you hold me in your arms
And say baby please don't cry
But baby most of all
I guess I could say
You've always been with me
You've never gone far away

I love the way you talk with me
About the things both far and near
The way you look into my eyes
And tell if there are any tears
But baby I just hope
With all my heart and soul
That we will always be together

Because our love can always be better

I just love the way you talk to me
The way you hold your head and smile
Yes I just love the way you hold my hand
When you've been gone for little while
But baby most of all
I just love you plain and true
Cause baby when I'm with you
I just know I won't be blue

THE BEGINNING OF LOVE

From the first time I saw you
I felt a leap within my heart
A feeling I've never had before
When I felt love begin to start
But I held that feeling inside me
Because I knew that it could never be
The feeling that I was seeking
Was still too far from me

But as I sit here looking
Through this glass at you
I realize I was hoping
That all my dreams would come true
But you are like a star
Each night that disappears
Each time I try to touch you
You seem to bring nothing but tears

And as I realize
It's a goal I cannot reach
I don't feel too unhappy
About this little defeat
But I will go on believing
I will find my ship in the night
For I know within my heart
I will find someone to fill my heart

OUR TIME

Being with you is like having the entire world say I love you
For I never dreamed I could feel this way about anyone
Just talking to you feels my heart with desires I cannot describe
A feeling I thought only others could have

For you my dear are the one I've been waiting for all of my life
Someone I can talk too, share my life with and not worry about the outcome
For what we could share comes to people only once in a lifetime
For even without talking we touch each other in ways most only can imagine

For love is not just getting into bed, it is growing closer and closer as each day goes by
Being able to speak to each other without words
Being able to be there when all others have turned their back on you
For I now realize that being and becoming friends are the only way that true love comes to us

So believe me when I say you are the only one for me
Someone I'd be proud to take anywhere for anyone to meet
So I say to you we only have one life to live
So let's not waste time trying not to believe this could happen to us

For like you I too have fears about closeness and the feelings I have for you
So let's take a chance and share what we have together
For tomorrow is not promise and yesterday is gone
For two people working together can build a life that no one can tear apart
So let's go for the gold, and be happy with the life we can share together

YOU ARE THE ONE

As I am lying in my bed thinking of you
I can still picture your sweet smile
The way you move when you walk
The sound of your voice as we talk
For you girl have stolen my heart
Put the fire back in my life
Made me feel like a man is supposed to feel

For a woman can make or break a man
For she along has the power to help a man become what he's supposed to be
And you my love make me feel like I can do anything
Climb the highest mountain
Swim the deepest sea without fear of failing
Yes you are the one I want in my life
The one that can make everything all right
For when you are not around I feel emptiness
That makes me hurt to breathe
I cannot think right, nor sleep right for always thinking of you

Wanting you in my arms to hold you tight
Kissing you all over until your body is on fire
Loving you until you are completely satisfied
And when we are finished, to love you all over again
For I will never want you to go
As long as there is breathe in my body

Yes my love I count the hours until we meet again
Until we can make love over and over again
For us two were meant for each other
For we are like a bee and honey
Never to part for a long time
Yes one without the other cannot survive
So my love hear me what I have to say

For it is from my heart, never let us part

IS THIS FOR REAL?

It's hard for me to understand the things that are in your mine
Are the things you feel on a rainy day when words are so hard to find?
I hope one day we will be together with both understanding and love
Because I hold a special feeling in my heart and it can only be a thing called love
As I think of you as each day goes by I begin to wonder what this is all about
For you my love is an only love that I only used to dream about
This feeling that we're talking about I know in my heart how I feel
Because without you here standing beside me I cannot face another day
So I hope in my heart that all this is real and we will be happy for a long, long time
Because baby you're the only one that I ever would want to be with till the end of time

SUNSHINE IN DARKNESS

Sometimes I wonder what it is all about
But then I look at you and know
Because you are someone who inspires me
Someone who helps me make it through each day
Without you everyday would be blue
The sun would no longer shine
It would be as if someone stole my heart
But with you I can make it
Because I have the inspiration to do something
To make something of myself
To make us a better life
All I need is you by my side
I would have the moon, the stars, and everything
We can make the rich seem poor
We can make the sun seem dull
Yes, lady you are special
That's why I want you, I need you, and I love you
So each time you read this just think here is someone who cares
Someone who will love you always
Just you and I until the end time

IS SHE REALLY GONE?

To lose that special someone you love
Is like carrying a heavy load
It's like losing a best friend
That used to help you carry that heavy load
It's like all your days are filled with rain
The brightness of the day is gone
You no longer enjoy anything

It's like all your happiness is gone
All you want to do is be left alone
To settle all your fears in tears
You just don't know what to do with yourself
You just sit there all alone with your fears
When she closes the door
You thought it was only for a little while
But as the time went on
You realize it was going to be quite awhile

But you still hold on to that hope
That she will come back to you
Because you have all the love to give her
To keep her from ever feeling blue
But as the days turn to months
You know that she will never be back again
But you know if she walks through that door
You would always be ready to take her back again
But it is still hard to lose that special love
And try to start life all over again

LOVE

Love is something you can't explain
You can only feel it within your heart
A feeling that grows as each day goes by
And never seems to part
One can love so many things
And yet have but one true love
Yes, love can be so many things
And be as different as each star above
But once you find that one true love
Your day will turn a rosy hue
And you will find you can do so many things
And it's all up to you

Yes the love of a woman
Is a powerful thing
And you must treat it with tender loving care
Cause once you lose that special love
You'll always live to shed a tear
Love can make you happy
And also make you blue
But whatever feeling you have
It's entirely up to you
Yes love is a wonderful thing
That everyone should live to enjoy
And without that feeling in this world
It might just as well be destroyed

THE FEELINGS OF LOVE

The love in my heart for you
Is hard to explain
It grows more and more as each day goes by
It's like the beginning of warm fire that flows all over
It's something that you can't turn off and on
The feeling just grows each time I see you
Sometimes I am so filled with love for you
I just want to take wings and fly high to the sky
It fills me with a feeling of belonging to someone
Of sharing all her hopes and fears
A feeling I just can't explain to anyone
Sometimes it fills me with great pain
But it is the pain of happiness
Sometimes I wouldn't trade this feeling for all the money in the world
It's worth more than all the gold in the world
More than anything you could ever own
More than the good taste of food
More than a good cold drink on a hot day
Yes this love I have for you is something
I will not give it up
It's something I want to last forever
I know it will last forever in my heart
Each time I think of you I get a warm feeling in my heart
A feeling that seems to brighten up my whole day
And when I see you I can't explain how I feel
It's like I just want to touch you for just a little while
Yes little girl of mine our love will last until the end of time
Until there's no one left but me and you
So let's hold on to what we have
And just be happy till each of us goes to a higher land above
Just you and me together until the end of our time

THE PAINS OF LOVE

Love is something two people try to find to build their lives together
An emotion that has been known to have everlasting staying power
An emotion that can offer happiness and enjoyment for many years to come
It can fill the heart with joy and make you feel all is well with the world
Once love has entered your life there is love for everyone and everything in life
Your days are filled with thoughts and wonderment of another
Your nights are filled with love talk and lovemaking with another
When you are in love with another all is well with the world
You feel that no hurt or pain can touch you as long as you have love from another
For God has sent you the one person who fills all your dreams of love

Love is something two people try to find to build their lives together
However, when only one person has the love it is not a happy tune
For they are always hoping and praying that their mate will catch up soon
And it will not be too long, for life ends far too soon
You spent your days in agony and you have many a sleepless night
For you feel that your true love will sometimes never see the light
You wonder what you can do to help her along the way
But you know in your heart that this is a decision she must make in her own way
You pray to God and ask Him what you ought to do
But you know in your heart there's nothing that He can do unless the love is true

Love is something two people try to find to build their lives together
But love is something that comes in and out throughout our life
And it is not easy to find for it can be painful in many ways
Sometimes we lose our way and do not trust the love we feel
And lose a love meant for us that have kept us happy for many years

Sometimes the pains of past relationships keep us blind in our today
And the true love meant for us will go sailing slowly away
So we must keep our hearts and minds open for love to come
For is but a short moment in time for love to be our friend

CARING

Sometimes I wonder if you really care
Because I know in my heart
That I really love you
I love you so much baby it hurts
Every time I think of you
I think of someone who is very dear to me
I think of a love that cannot be cured
A love that no other man can compete with
But I know baby that you love me too
Even though sometimes baby
You treat me really, really bad
You say things that really hurt
Even though you don't mean them
But at least do one thing for me
Think before you say the things that hurt
That way you know baby you and me
Will be together till times get better
Until the sun no longer shines
Until mankind no longer exists
So baby let's stop all this nonsense
And be happy everyday
Let no man or woman come between us

TOGETHER

Even though we just met
I have a feeling within my heart
And as we get to know each other better
I hope we will never have to part
I know have found a woman
Who will stand beside me in future days?
A woman who will give me her love
Even though she doesn't know my many ways
Each day I read your letters
I understand you a little more
Because I know that you are a warm and sweet person
I've never met a woman like you before
And I count the days until you come see me
And brighten up my whole day
Yes woman you are the love of my life
The beginning of a brand new day
It's hard for you to believe these words, I know
Because you've heard them many times before
But just have a little trust in me
And we won't worry about times before
It won't be long till I am free
And we can be together for the first time
But I know in my heart things will work
And we'll be together for a long, long, time

DEDICATED TO MY SISTER MADELINE PATRICIA EDWARDS

1950 - 1986

Losing a sister or any family member to death is one of the hardest feelings to deal with on this earth, but with God's help you can.

THERE IS NO PAIN IN DEATH

Though you have lost a loved one and you are filled with pain and grief, do not be in despair
The Lord has taken them home where there is no more pain and misery
No more sickness or darkness, only light shines at this time
For He has taken them to house in the heavens for peace and happiness

The Lord does not want you to mourn for the death of a loved one
Because they are through with their suffering and have found peace in His Kingdom
So be happy for the one who has gone home, for you will not see them again until it is your time
For we all must go and see the Lord one day and not suffer on this earth forever

God is great and merciful; He let His Son die for us so that we might be saved when we die
So that we would have a home to go to after all our days are done on this earth
So be thankful when He takes them, for they have a happiness that we can never know while we are here
So cry a little; then be thankful that they have gone home to see the Lord for eternity

TRUST IN THE LORD

When the Lord comes to get you, you shouldn't be afraid
No more pain, no more sorrow, only happiness in your life
So put your trust in the Lord and He will never let you down
Put your trust in the Lord and He'll lead you to his Holy Ground

There's so much trouble in this world no one seems to care
When you call on the Lord you know He'll always be there and you know that He will always care
So put your trust in the Lord and He will never let you down
Put your trust in the Lord and He'll lead you to His Holy Ground

So when your loved one is gone, don't be in pain and misery
Because they've gone to His Kingdom to be happy and live free
So out your trust in the Lord and He will never let you down
Put your trust in the Lord and He'll lead you to His Holy Ground

DEATH IS NOT THE END

Many people are afraid of death, because they don't understand what it is all about.
For death is not the end, as most people think.
It is only the beginning of life as we cannot know it.
For when God blew the breath of life in man that was not all. He also blew His spirit into man; which we call The Holy Spirit.
When each of us is born we have it in us.
And when God wants you to hear Him, He speaks through The Holy Spirit.

Before Jesus came there was no life after death, because God had condemned most men on this earth not to see or hear Him, but He had a few that could.
So being a merciful God, He sent His only Son down here to die so that we could be free of all our sin's of the flesh. By God doing this we could have life after our flesh has died.
When you are afraid of death Satan loves it, because it keeps you from knowing how Good God has been to you.
Death is not to be feared, for it is only the beginning of a new life with our Father and His SON in Heaven and the Promise Land.
For when the body stops breathing, our spirit lives on.
Then God will look in His Book of Life to see if you have lived the kind of life He wanted you to live.
If you haven't, then the fires of Hell you will see.

So while you are here live the kind of life God wants you to live.
Follow in Jesus' footsteps, for He has already made a path for you to follow with plenty of light, and if you stay on that path you can be Save.
So be not afraid, death cannot hurt you if you believe in our Lord Jesus, and that He died on the Cross and shed His blood for you and me, all will be well.

NO USE FIGHTING

Jesus saves, Jesus saves. He died on that cross for you and me.
He shed His blood so that we might see the Kingdom of Heaven when we leave here.
There is no other you can turn to when you are down and out.
You can try to deny Him, but we know in our hearts that He is there.
He is there when we need Him, even when others aren't.
All He asks is that you love Him and do the things you know are right.
Don't be afraid of the things He lets you see, because they bring no harm to you.
When He calls you to come, He will not be denied.
He wants you to love people as you love Him and yourself.
Help someone when they are down, even if it is your worst enemy.
Always try to find something good in everyone; even your enemy could turn out to be your best friend.
For there is no running from Jesus when he puts something for you to do in your heart
He doesn't want you to live a life of hate, or of past memories.
Live for now, for yesterday is gone, and tomorrow may never come.
If you have the love of Jesus in your heart, it will show and help others to know that He can change them too
For His love is like no other; so stop fighting the Lord and let Him into your heart and live happy while you are here

GOING HOME

When the Lord comes to get you, you shouldn't be afraid
Because He knows you're so tired, and He's carrying you home to stay

Close your eyes and sleep my child, because you're going home to stay.
There will be no more sadness only happiness and joy every day

When the Lord comes to get you, you shouldn't be afraid
Because He knows you're so tired, and He's carrying you home to stay

So don't you weep when they leave you, they are only going home to stay
To God's house in the Heavens, where only peace prevails

When the Lord comes to get you, you shouldn't be afraid
Because He knows you're so tired, and He's carrying you home to stay

So be happy for your loved ones when they have gone away
They'll be happy in the Heavens, because Jesus Christ is there

So when the Lord comes to get you, you shouldn't be afraid
Because He knows you are tired, and He's carrying you home to stay

THE LORD IS REAL

Yes I love you in my heart tonight; I love you in my life today
And this feeling that I have it never goes away because the love in my heart is real

My Lord is Jesus; I love Him more each day
And one day when I'm gone I'm going home to my Lord's Kingdom far away

Each day when I pray I thank the Lord for coming into my life
I know He is real the way He makes me feel by the love I have in my heart for Him today

My Lord is Jesus I love Him more each day
And one day when I'm gone I know I'm going to my Lord's Kingdom far away

Lord help me please to let others know what's really in my heart
For if they only knew how you make me feel they would let you into their heart too

My Lord is Jesus I love him more each day
And one day when I'm gone I know I'm going home to my Lord's Kingdom far away

FOR ALL THE WOMEN
WHO MAKE LIFE GREAT

Women are to be loved and taken care of for all times. For they can inspire you to be the best that you can be and make you feel that life is a wonderful place to be on this earth.

BEAUTIFUL BLACK WOMAN

Looking at you is like looking at a rainbow after a soft summer rain
So full of life and wonderment, beauty and grace, that fills my heart with a need to be with you
To hold you, to touch you, to protect you from any danger that life has to offer
To sweep you off your feet and take you to a land that will be only ours
A land where all your dreams, hopes, and desires can be fulfilled at a moment's notice
A place where there is no darkness, only light, a place where only happy lovers go
Where all things are possible if you believe in them hard enough
Where there is no unhappiness, only life to be enjoyed forever and a day
Where the air smells like roses, and the water taste like fresh honeydew

Yes, you are the essence of a beautiful black woman whose looks goes far beyond the top surface
For your beauty shines through even when you are trying not to let anyone see it
For when I am there talking with you there is no outside world
Only us sharing our dreams, hopes, and fears, and hoping that our love will survive
Trying to get to know one another, trying to form a bond that cannot be broken by the outside world
Trying to grow and become the best persons that we can be while on this earth
And trying to show others that two people can learn to live with each other's faults
Being able to talk to each other about any and everything, no matter how mad we become at each other
To show that love is not just sex, but understanding, patience, and growing as individuals

Yes, to share my love with you is like winning millions of dollars in the lottery
It's like climbing the highest mountain and shouting to the world that love is real
That if you find that one person there is nothing to fear in this life
For you will always have that one special person in your life who will never let you down
Yes, my beautiful black woman, that one person is you and you alone, that I want to share my life with
For you inspire me to be the best that I can be in this life, and I will do the same for you
For together we can conquer anything this life has to offer on this earth
So come, let us go forward in this life together and show the world a love that grows forever
A love that cannot be stopped, because we will make it last no matter what life throws at us

SURFACE BEAUTY

Some men look at a woman and think what a beautiful woman to behold
Not realizing that her heart is devastated and there is much weeping inside
They look at her beautiful brown eyes and think I wish they were looking at me
Not wanting to see that those brown eyes are filled with tears and about to cry from sorrow
Men looking at those lips and wondering if they could have but one kiss for a short while
Not seeing the grimace on those lips that are saying that they have not the time to play
Looking at that beautiful face and thinking that all is well in life and nothing can go wrong
Not realizing someone has just told her that she not welcome in their life anymore
Telling her that she is no longer their best friend and to go away and leave them along forever
Can they not see that this woman needs a friend at this time not someone that wants to use her?
A friend to talk with and let go of her emotions and release this pain inside that hurts so bad
Can her man not see that he has lost a friend and someone that would be with him for all time?

Be not in despair at this time of hurt and pain in your life for your tears will one day be no more
You think that love will never come your way and you will not share your heart for evermore
All men are not to be trusted and you want to crush them and make them feel the pain you feel
You want them to feel the loneliness that you feel each night before you are able to sleep

To weep on and on into their pillow and their heart fills with ache they think will never go away
Be not in despair for these feelings that you have will one day pass and you will forget this pain
And the sun will shine and bring an end to those days filled with happiness, despair and agony
For there is a man out there that will love you and show you the respect that you want in life
A man that will be your best friend and share his whole body and soul with you for all days to come
Someone that will fill your days will with sunshine not tears, pain and grief to bring you down
That will love you for all the days of this life, no matter if the days are filled with sunshine or rain
So be of good cheer my beautiful woman for when your life is filled with pain, sunshine is never far behind

NO ONE LIKE YOU

When I first saw you I realized that you were someone special
Someone a man could learn to love forever
Someone who is a caring and sharing person, and who would make a man happy for the rest of his life
That winning smile would melt even the coldest man's heart
So that he would give you anything just to make you happy
To keep you safe from any danger that would come your way
To make the whole world bow down to your every need
When you look at me with those beautiful eyes of yours
I feel as if you could see my every thought and know my every pain
And know that I really want you in my life, so that we grow and learn to love each other.

Yes, Lady you are the one for me, the one I need to make me a whole person
So come with me so that we can share our lives together
And not worry about the ups and downs of the outside world
For when we are alone together nothing can touch us
We can talk, laugh, and even cry together while we are sharing these special moments
Knowing that no matter what happens we will always be there for one another
Always to know that as long as we grow together and become one, nothing can tear us apart
So come and go with me on this adventure that I want to take you on
And your life will never be the same again
For this adventure is one of love, one of excitement, and one that will give you riches, that in this world you sometimes never find

THINKING OF YOU

You are a woman who has abundant beauty and grace
And in everything you do, it's done with taste
You have such beautiful eyes that sparkle when you're merry
And when you smile at me I become so very, very happy
For your smile would light up a room and shine like the moon above
And in everything you do people would know that you have been well read
I'm glad that I have met you and that you are a part of my life
And I hope that once you know me we will not have a lot of strife
For I want you in my life, for I know that we could make it
And lady you need not worry for your heart, I would not break it

I would give you the moon and the stars if the good Lord would allow it
And make all your dreams come true, for Lady I think you deserve it
I would wipe away your tears and never make you sad
And In all the things I do, I intend to make you very, very glad
For there is nothing on this earth that you should not have
And there should be nothing on this earth that should ever make you sad
So when you are feeling blue and don't know what to do
Just call me anytime, and I will do anything to keep you from feeling blue
Yes you are the woman who can fulfill all my dreams
And I will try to fulfill yours by any and every means

Yes my love, my heart, please never ever let me down
For I don't want to be the one going around wearing a frown
For I want us always to be happy in everything we say and do
And I don't want us to ever be going around feeling blue
I want us to have the best that all this life has to offer
And I want us to have it before we end up in a walker
I want us to be together forever until the end of time
And share our love together in front of all mankind
And so my love if you will have me and share all my love
I swear that I will be with you until Heaven calls us from up above

BLACK AND BEAUTIFUL

Every black woman has her own grace and style to match her beauty
You my dear have much to offer a man who has the opportunity to look upon your beauty
For to look into those beautiful eyes of yours is to fill my soul with joy and happiness
It is like looking at the moon with the entire glow that fills the night sky with brightness
For I see in you a woman who would make any man a good friend and more
The look of a woman who is sure of what she wants in this life and goes out to obtain it
A woman who when she steps into a room all eyes turn to see who this person is and want to be near her
They wonder if they might have the chance to meet this person and fill her inner circle of friends
For she lights all these that are around and will make those that are in her world even better for being there
You are the Queen Bee who inspires all the workers inside the hive to work so that all will enjoy the honey
Yes, you are the one people want in their lives and want to be friends with forever and ever, no matter what

Yes black woman you are the one who men want when they daydream about the woman they would like in their lives
The one they dream about when they want the pleasure of a beautiful woman at their side whenever they are out and about
Yes, just being around you brings sunshine into any man's world and lights up the possibility of love
They wonder what it would be like just to have one kiss from these beautiful well, shaped-lips of yours
To receive a hug that fills their whole body and soul with happiness of having a chance of being with your everyday of their lives
To know that if you are in their corner you will not turn your back on them as long they treat you with love and respect

They know that to being together with you mean a lifetime of happiness and love that will last forever and a day
To know that together there are no mountains that cannot be climbed or a road that is not successful with you in their life
Yes, my black woman you are the one who lights up men heart and inspire them to do better with their lives
Yes, my black woman stay as sweet and desirable as you are now for all the days of your life
For you will be able to bless all who come into your life with much happiness and love for all of their lives

CHRISTMAS

Christmas, a time we rejoice in for the birth of Christ on this earth. For those who believe it means that we can have ever- lasting life in the Promise Land once we leave this earth.

CHRISTMAS SPIRIT

Christmas is the time of year where sometimes people seem to forget, that this is the time of giving and spreading God's love to every heart
We put so much into receiving gifts and Santa bringing kids lots of toys that Jesus takes a back seat and we drown Him out with lots of noise
We do a lot of eating and drinking with family and friends and we soon forget that there are people out there looking for someone to be their best friend
They are hungry and they are tired and they need a place to stay, but sometimes people turn their backs on them for they are afraid of what others might say
They judge that all are nothing more than drunks and drug addicts
 But most of the people out there are just like you and me they need a place to stay and their children a yard to play
Most are down on their luck or have lost a job and all they are asking for is a fair chance for another job
Some took their kids and run from the abusive homes and ask for nothing in return except for a fair chance to start again
While others are service men and women who are down on their luck and are only asking for a second chance at a life?
But Christ sits in the back seat waiting to be called

Christmas can be the time of year when the thefts come out at night and suicide has its way, because of the broken dreams of many
Stores take advantage of people, marking up their prices and abused children go on dying, while the hungry go on crying
People pretend to celebrate the coming of Christ and to bring joy to the world, while men are always making plans for the beginning of war
To take over a country with bloodshed and tears, and teach our way of living with bloodshed and fear
For we seem to forget the spirit of Christmas as we think about only our needs and leave others to suffer and tell them to get upon the knees and pray

For the light in our lives have grown dim and weak, so we try to make sure that others lights go out
The politicians go home to celebrate the many blessing they have received, while the hungry working poor are crying in their in sleep
They celebrate the many gifts they bring to family and the food that will be prepared, while many others sit on the street with nothing but despair
But Christ sits in the back seat waiting to be called

Christmas is the birthday of Jesus born into this world to die on the cross so that all our sins could be forgiven as He hung upon that cross?
He did not die, upon the cross so that we could eat and drink and be merry
He died upon that cross so that our souls would not be weary
He did not died upon that cross so that we could be selfish and not give to others, He died so that all men and women on earth could be saved and spread His love to others
We are here on this earth to help our friends and neighbors and to make sure all peoples are taken care of all year round
Jesus is the light we need throughout each and every year, but sometimes we think more about receiving gifts and being selfish and forget about Jesus light at this time of the year
We sometimes think we are the only ones suffering at Christmas, but forget there are many out there like us with the need of Jesus in our hearts
There are many out there suffering during Christmas holidays, but if we open our hearts and minds like Jesus we can make everyone's Christmas a wonderful day
People do not always need food and drink to make Christmas a beautiful day, what they really need is the love of Jesus each and everyday
But Christ sits in the back seat waiting to be called

CHRISTMAS SPREAD EVERYWHERE

Christmas is the time of year for the joyous celebration of our Savior Jesus Christ and the love that we can spread upon each other each and everyday
The sound of children's laughter as they open up gifts of toys and playing with family and friends spreading all their joy
Of people showing love for all the world to see and not expecting anything, but the joy of love from all others on this perfect day
Family and friends enjoying fellowship with lots of games and fun, praying that all the world will be doing the very same and having lots of fun
It is the time of year where one is not afraid to start a new life and know that Jesus and friends are there to help you win this fight
For your family life has begun to shine and your problems seem so far away and you have a chance at a life that you thought was long since gone
For Jesus has helped you see that everyone is not the same and that there are people out there who are willing to be your friend
There are people out there that will show you a brand new way and help you win whatever battles will come upon your way
For Christmas time is for giving and love among your friends and the time of year where family should all join hands as friends
To set the table with lots of food and sweets and to invite those who have no family and friends to help through the night
To show the world that Christmas is more than just receiving gifts and having fun, that Christmas is the time of year where Jesus has always won
Yes Christmas comes but once a year and love is in the air, but Christmas should be all year round with love spread everywhere

THE SPIRIT OF CHRISTMAS IS IN YOUR HEART

Christmas is not the time of year to rejoice in sending money or gifts for others and hope you receive yours
Christmas is not the time of year to worry about what sales are on so you can spend less
Christmas is not the time of year to sing about Santa Claus and the reindeer coming to deliver presents to your kids
Christmas is not for making you feel guilty because you have nothing and no family
Christmas is not for feeling sorry for yourself and wanting not to live life to the fullest
Christmas is not the time for your heart to be filled with pain and jealousy for others who have more than you
Christmas is not the time to go out and take what others have so that your Christmas will be better
Christmas is not the time to get drunk and full of drugs and kill the spirit of Christmas for others just because you hate yourself
Christmas is not the time to stop believing in Jesus just because you do not have everything you want in this life

Christmas is the time of the year to rejoice in Jesus' birth and the saving of your soul when you leave this earth
Christmas is about giving to those who have not and not expecting any gifts in return for what you have done
 Christmas is about the joy your heart should feel when you think of Jesus on this holy day of days
Christmas is about families getting together and rejoicing that they are alive and well for another year to celebrate this day
Christmas is about teaching your kids that gift giving is to celebrate the birth of Jesus as the Three Wise Men did
Christmas is about teaching your kids to love all human beings, no matter who they are and where they came from

Christmas is about knowing that no matter what anyone tells you Jesus is the only one who can lead you to the promise land once you leave this earth

Christmas is about the world getting together and realizing there is but one God, and He does not cause confusion

Christmas is about believing in your mind, body, and soul that there is but one person who can save you, and His name is Jesus

ST NICK IN THE GHETTO

It was the night before Christmas way down in the ghetto
Where the parents were partying on their bottles of Ripple
And the children were upstairs lying in their beds
And wondering what the noise was about downstairs
They wondered if St. Nick would dare to appear
Or would the noise downstairs make him disappear
They wondered how he would ever get in
Since there was no chimney in what they called a den
Then one kid yells out have no fear
When St. Nick comes in I'll usher him right up here
He'll lay the toys out while you all are asleep upstairs
And when you wake up you're all have a treat
But as the night went on their eyelids got heavy until they were all asleep
Dreaming of St. Nick bringing in all their bevy

Meanwhile downstairs the party was over
All heading home to a wait on their hangovers
As father headed upstairs to get into bed
He heard a loud yell out in the yard with plenty of bells
As he looked out the window he couldn't believe his eyes
For there sat a dozen reindeer in a black and white sleigh
With a jolly fat black man all dress up in red
Father looked up to Heaven and asked "Oh God am I dead
Or am I up stairs dreaming in my nice warm bed?
Old St. Nick jumped off the large sleigh
And picked up his hat and covered his head
And reached into the sleigh and took out his bag
And as he turned around a toy soldier jumped out of the bag
Happily weaving an African American Flag
As old St. Nick came up to the door
My father keeled over and hit the wood floor

The door to the house open to let him in

And he stepped over my father who was lying in the middle of the floor
And in flash He laid toys everywhere all shining and new
Waiting for the happy look of kids playing with toys on the morns, early dew
For He had no time to waste there were lots of ghettos to cover
And lots of toys to deliver in the deep night of cover
He even had time to have a piece of Mom's Carmel cake
This put a smile on His face and an extra step in his gait
He leaps into His sleigh and said "boys let's get going
We have lots of places to cover before dawns' early morn
And off into the night went this jolly black man
For He knew in His heart He had a good plan

As father woke up he made his way back to the window
To see if this was a dream or a great miracle of wonder
And as he looked up to see St. Nick waved with a smile
He said Merry Christmas to all who have seen me tonight
For the kids will awaken up with all their dreams fulfilled
And throughout the ghetto all parents will know that St. Nick has been here

DIFFERENT THOUGHTS ABOUT LIFE ON THIS EARTH

Thoughts about life as we go through live on this earth and see the world from our point of view and sometimes wonder how humans have survived this long.

THE POWER OF A VISIT

It's hard to wait for someone you love
The minutes seem to turn to hours
Just as a day can seem like a week
It seems she can't get here fast enough
It's like no other day in the week
But you wait those many minutes
Hoping that she will be here soon
Because in your heart you will be glad to see her
Even if it takes all day or even tomorrow afternoon
Because a visit is very special
Especially if that right lady comes
She can brighten up your day
And it makes your time seem to run

But if she does not come
You are sitting here wondering why
Because in your heart you are hoping
You didn't do anything to make her cry
Because if you did you are hoping
She will come back again
So you can try to make it all up to her
That way you can start all over again
Because in your heart you know you love her
And you'll always want her back again
Because there is no one like her in the world
That could ever make you happy again

So if you get that visit
Try not to say all the wrong things
And try to keep her happy
That way you'll always have a happy ending

LONELY

To be lonely is a hell of a thing
Not having anyone to talk to
Not being able to confined in anyone
Just being alone by yourself
But having someone who is only there in spirit with you
Can be just as lonely as the day before

Not being able to see her
To play those little games you and she had in common
Not having those little talks
Not being able to tell her how much you really care
To worry about life together
Yes, to have someone with you
To face life many problems
Is a very good thing to have?
That's why when she's not there
You have a lot of time to think
A lot of time to feel how much you really miss her
How much you don't really want to be without her
But most of all you wonder if she cares as much for you
Does she feel those lonely pains of wanting to be next to you?
To whisper those sweet love words in your ear
Does she really have that feeling of love, or is it just a dream
Where you wake up and find she's not there?

Then you will have that lonely ache again
A feeling I hope no one will ever have to have
Because being lonely is very hard
That's why I hope little lady of mine
We will never let that happen to us again

BEING LOST

The love of a good woman is hard to find, because first you have to love yourself
Love is something that grows more as each day goes by.
You have to work at it, just like anything else
Sometimes you have to give more then you get, but if you have the right woman it's really all worthwhile
Two people working toward the same goal can do wonders
You have to know yourself before you can see the love anyone else has to offer you
Once you get sober you can see a lot; you can see what a mess you have made of your life while you were drinking
You can see how wrong you were about a lot of little things
How you abused people; how you didn't care about anyone but yourself, and you really didn't care about you
You only thought you did

You always thought you knew everything, but you really didn't know anything
All you knew how to do was to keep trying to kill yourself and wanting everyone to suffer with you while you were doing it
Then something happened, a voice said," get help, call someone and get help while there's still time and hear what people have to say, Instead of always talking
For the first time in your life you heard what people were saying, and now you have found happiness by being sober
With the help of God, He has let you discover a beautiful, wonderful woman
So, what else do you need to stay sober?

I'm so glad I listened to that voice inside of me when it said, "get help," and anyone can have it if they want it
You just have to listen to God, and a lot of good people helping you

FOREVER

Forever is a space and place of time that no one can define
Some people count it by days and weeks
But I count it as a state of mind
For how can you count anything in days and weeks?
When it's nothing but a vanishing memory
From a thought that was in your mind
That you thought you wanted to last for all times

The reason I say all this
Is because it can be no other way
For how can you define a space of time?
That never seems to stay
It's just like a man and woman
Who thought they were in love
They said that their love would last forever

But then one day it happens in time
All the love they had is gone
But in their minds they still have memory of love
Although the love is not as strong
They still think that it can last till the end
And they still believe they can run away
And keep their love strong, even though it is the end

That's why I say forever is a state of mind
Or is it just a lingering memory
And though you might not feel the same
About the many things you've had
You can retain them in your mind
And being them back when you feel sad
And make them last to the end of time

WHERE IS GOD?

From the time that we are first born we begin to learn about God
They tell us He is real and will always be on our side
They tell us He is strong and can never do any wrong
And in the end, if you are in the right you will always win
They say that He knows everything and see's everything you do
And no matter where you hide He will always be able to find you
They say that He is all powerful and created us one and all
And that no matter what you say or do He will never let you fall
They say that God is merciful and forgives us all our sins
And that He will love you with all His heart, for sinners are His best friends
They say that Christ was born to make our burdens light
And in the end when we are gone He will to take us to a higher height
They say that when you pray He will grant your heart's desire
And never let you wonder if you are going to the Lake of Fire
Yes, God is everything to everyone who keeps all His Laws and Rules
And He will make sure that you are never left looking like a fool

But I'm from the ghetto and live on the poorer side of town
And the God I know seems to be always wearing a frown
I see nothing but death and distortion in every day of my life
With no hope for all these souls that are crying in the night
I hear the hungry children crying from the abuse that they must take
And God sits on His Throne never caring or doing anything about their fate
I hear the women praying and asking God for just a little help
They might as well be silent from the answers that they get
I hear the grown men saying that they will always do God's will
But in the end I always hear them say that killing is the only way to do God's will

I pray and I pray to God to get answers about all that's going on
But it seems to me He's always busy, or He's always away from home
In the church the minister's say that they can show us God's way
But it seems to me that all they get do is nothing, but get in God's way
They say they have these visions from God who sits high up above
But in the end all they do is make sure you pay the money that's due

So as I look across this land to see if I can find God
I see nothing but death and suffering that makes me so very tired
I see no hope and caring that God even made a dent upon man's mind
I see no hope for the children to be relieved from all their crying
Where is this God of hope whom men preach about in all our lives?
Where is this God of hope whom women are praying to while they are kneeling?
Where is this God of hope who promised to be there when you need Him?
Where is this God of hope when despair and misery is your best friend?
Could it be that this has all been a lie to keep people in their place?
Or is God just waiting to show us who He is in the right time and place?
Could it be that we've been fooled with illusions and dreams?
Or is God just waiting to fulfill all our every needs?
Whatever the case may be I just hope and pray in the end
That God is true a friend and will not fail me and be my friend

THE ROAD OF UNHAPPINESS

There are many things in life that people shouldn't know
That most of the time only make them sad and lonely
It will only keep them down and always keep you going round and round
Yes, that's what drinking will do to most people; even though they don't know it yet
It will keep the money out of your pockets, and you always will be poor
Your home life will be a wreck, for you are always making a mess
Your love life will be like a merry-go-round, and you will always be dizzy
There is never a beginning or end and any there to be your friend
You think you are doing the right thing but you are always doing wrong
Most of all it will give you no rest, no peace of mind at all
Yes, it's like a sky that has no ending and the moon that doesn't shine
It fills your world with darkness and the lights are always so far away
So if you have that chance not to drink take my advice and don't waste your time
It will only lead you down a road of unhappiness, sorrow and pain in the end
So be happy the way you are, and be thankful for what you've got on this earth
For a drinking man's life like a sinking ship a road that has no end
A life that's no life at all and will only make you wish that you had stopped before you began

YOU CANNOT WIN

Oh Death! Oh Death! Why do you treat us so mean?
You take away our life just when we thought we had escaped
You fill our dreams with fear, and we wake up with a start;
We never know where you are or when you'll take us down
You stay among the shadows, just out of our sight
By the time that we see you it's too late to take flight
For to run would mean nothing, for you are always ahead of the game
The cards that you hold in your hands are filled with all our names

Oh Death! Oh Death! Why do you treat us so mean?
You take away our young before they can grow old
You take away our old and make them so very, very cold
Just when we think we're on top of the world with all our wealth and fame
You come into our windows before we can make our claim
You slowly creep up on us and wrap us in your arms
And take us into nothingness before we can sound an alarm
And suddenly our life is gone before we can even make a run
Just like someone trying to fire back, with nothing but an empty gun

Oh Death! Oh Death! Why do you treat us so mean?
We fear you in our waking hours, and even when we're asleep
We fear you most of all, because we know you can't be beat
Where do you take us when you wrap us in your arms of death?
Is it to a another place where we can have a better life
Or is to a place where life is finally done?
I know not when you'll come for me or when my name will be called
I know that when you come I cannot avoid this fall
So we the people of this earth need not worry about death
Just enjoy your life while you can, for death will always be there ready to make his call

CRY MY CHILDREN, CRY

Cry my children, cry, for the world watched you while you die
They watch and said nothing as you are used and abused
As they did while Hitler was slaying the Jews
They say they will protect you from all hurt and harm
But in reality they pretend like they don't know what's going on
They listen to your cries at night as you are being beaten
They tell you that you will go to hell form all the lies and weeping
And as you run away from all the beatings you've had
They tell you, you ought to be glad for the little that you have

Cry my children, cry, for the world watched you while you die
You dream of parents who will love you no matter what
But you have the type of parents who are always committing a crime
They are never happy with you know no matter what you say and do
Sometimes you wonder why the hell God made you, for you are always feeling blue
They send you to school to get an education
But when you get home you can't get a decent conversation
God won't you hear this child who is crying in his sleep
Sometimes I feel a like little Bo Peep, who lost all her sheep.

Cry my children; cry for the world watched you while you die
I have prayed and prayed again for God to hear the many cries
But the only results I see is that a lot more children have died
I'm afraid to go to sleep at night for fear I will be beat
And left to die in a pool of blood like a burned out field of wheat
I think that one day while they sleep that I will kill them all
For it really doesn't matter I've heard the Devil's call
So when you come home at night and see you children playing
Why don't you go somewhere and do you a little praying?

TOMORROW

Many is the day I wish that tomorrow would never come
Many is the day I knew that sometimes I would fall when I began to run
Many is the day that I asked why is my mother crying
Many are the day that I knew that many people would start dying
Many is the day that I wish that all was well with the world
Many is the day that that I knew I was not fast enough to caught a squirrel
Many is the day that I wish that people would learn not to hate
Many is the day that I knew that crime would never take a hike
Many is the day that I wish I could join the birds in flight
Many are the day that I knew that the government would never stop the fight
Many is the day that I wish that children could have fun all the days of their life
Many is the day that I knew that people would teach them how to take a life

Many is the day that I wish that tomorrow would never come
Many is the day that I knew that some governments would kill just for fun
Many is the day that I wish that children would not be abuse while growing up
Many is the day that I knew that the children would not make it out of the hood
Many is that day that I wish I was anywhere in the world then where I am
Many is the day that I knew no matter where I was I might still be crying
Many is the day that I wish I had been born in a family that would not fight everyday
Many is the day that I knew that each family had to find its own way from day to day

Many is the day that I wish that the parents I had would disappear from this earth
Many is the day that I knew that one's parents might have thought the same way
Many is that the day that I wish that God would destroy this earth and start anew
Many is the day that I knew that human brings would destroy this earth again and make life blue

Many is the day I wish tomorrow would never come
Many is the day I knew tomorrow would always be on the run
Many is the day I wish that the government would always do its job
Many is the day I knew that it was impossible for this to happen at all
Many is the day I wish that hungry would disappear throughout the world
Many is the day I knew that this was a dream of a tree waiting to fall
Many is the day I wish that life was always simple and fair
Many Is the day that I knew it would be easier to have another world's fair
Many is the day I wish that all my dreams would come true while on this earth
Many is the day that I knew that it would be easier for a man to give birth
Many is the day I believed that God could save all the souls before we all die
Many is the day I knew that it would be easier to teach human brings to fly

POLITICS

Politics are like many little sledgehammers that come slowly down on your head, not enough to kill you
Enough to give you a migraine headache for the next two to four years when it is election time again.
Politics is the one sport that has no rules or referees to control what is going on with our government
The people only see what the politicians want them to see. It's like walking through a mine field blind.
It is better than a three-ring circus, with the president being the ringmaster
No clue as to what act is coming on next
However, he is always the star attraction when it comes to making a fool of himself
A politician says, "I'm going to help you keep your job
I'm going to take good care of you
Don't worry about a thing with me in office
"Trust me! Trust me! Trust me! "

Meanwhile, a man sits in his living room wondering who he will vote for in the next election for the office of president of the United States
The last four years he had helped to elect a Republican to fulfill this job
All it had gotten him was the lost of his job, because of the policy changes of the government The president had vetoed different bills that could have saved jobs from leaving this country
This time he decided he would vote for a Democrat for this office
With hope that the new president would get the people of this nation back to work
To keep the jobs from leaving this country
After the election the man spends four more years of being out of work.

Politics, the backbone of America, is also the heartbreak of America
For years Americans have believe in their government and politicians

For years the government and its politicians have slowly, but surely put America in debt
Children are hungry, people are dying, and the nation is crying, Help Us! Help Us! Help Us!
The politicians keep saying that times will get better
That good times are right around the next corner
Americans go to the polls to vote and pray like hell that their vote will set the nation right
All is lost, for the only things the politicians care about are, keeping their jobs
Lying to the people about what they really stand for and what they are going to do about the problems of the nation

    A baby is crying
    A politician is lying
    The man has lost has job
    The politicians are still lying
    The world is sighing
    The politicians are still lying
    A baby is dying
    A politician is lying, and lying, and lying

The many little sledgehammers come down with a mighty roar
The migraine headache is gone
The people are gone
The world is gone
Somewhere in the universe politicians lives on, and on, and on
For the chance to start a new government somewhere
To start the same old damned lies over and over again

CONCLUSION

I hope that you have enjoyed the poems in this book and have come away with a different outlook on life and the peoples thereof. For life is only what you make it and there is no since feeling sorry for yourself, for it is always better to get up off the ground and live life to its fullest.

Sometimes in this life you will find yourself in situations that will leave you questioning this life and the people that live on this earth. You might think there are folks in our government who care about the peoples of the United States, but some only care about having their job forever or until they died? In those times sit down and write something to yourself that is from the heart and inspirational to you and your family. For I have found there no better feeling than putting my words down on paper and reading them later in the day. This helps me to be less stressful in this life and help me to remember that there are many good people in this world and one most get to know the real person before one passes judgment on others. For even if God does not answer when you call or gives you everything you want in this life, He is always there when you need him.

Finally I would like to leave for your reading a paper I wrote some years ago. Hopefully it will give you food for thought, at the very least a look at life in a different light.

Write to you again soon

Melvin Avery Edwards

GOD, ALL POWERFUL?

It has been said that God is all-powerful, and that there is nothing that He cannot do. However, in regards to Evil, God seems not to have the power to destroy Evil even when he has a chance to, which would have share mankind a lot of suffering and heartache. Does this mean that God is not all powerful, and that He can only keep Evil from totally destroying mankind, and that Evil and God have the same power and one cannot do away with the other?

I shall attempt to show the possibility that God cannot totally eliminate Evil from the cosmos and that God can only stop Evil from running rampant on the face of the earth. I shall take three examples from the King James Bible and show that when confronted with Evil, and with a chance to destroy Evil, God chose to allow Evil to continue to cause harm and destruction on the earth and the cosmos, thus showing the possibility that God cannot eliminate Evil from the cosmos altogether.

However, I would like to say from the start that I am not using the King James Bible as an authority on God or as a fact based reference, nor am I saying that this paper is based on fact. It is a paper written by a lay person to show that the possibility exist that God does not have the power to eliminate Evil from the cosmos or from human brings lives, and that God can only act to mediate and control how far Evil can go to create harm to human beings and destruction to the cosmos.

Now it is said in the Bible that God created the cosmos and everything therein, thus He also created the Heavens and the earth. Upon creating the heavens He made the Angels that lived in Heaven, and He created Arch Angels that held leadership roles in the Angel population. The Arch Angels relayed messages from God to instruct the lower Angels on their everyday duties. However, according to the Bible there was one Arch Angel (Satan) that turned to Evil rather than Good, and tried to take over Heaven itself, and it says, (Rev 12:7-9) " And there was war in heaven: Michael and his Angels fought against the Dragon; and the Dragon fought and his Angels, And prevailed not;

neither was their place found any more in Heaven. The great Dragon was cast out, that old serpent, called the Devil, and/or Satan, which deceived the whole world: He was cast out into the earth, and His Angels were cast out with him."

You have just read God denounce this Arch Angel (Satan) by casting Him onto earth and giving Him <u>free will</u> to have the earth as His domain, along with the Angels that wanted to follow Him. Now in this situation God had three choices that he could have made:

1. He could have cast the evil out of this Arch Angel and restored him to a good angel.
2. He could have destroyed the Arch Angel and His follows, thus eliminating Evil right then.
3. He could have thrown the Arch Angel out of Heaven and allow him to spread His Evil to others.

Instead of casting the evil out of the Arch Angel and his follows, or eliminating the Evil altogether God chose to allow the Arch Angel and his follows to roam the earth and spread their evil ways upon the land and the life that lived upon this land called earth. Thus creating two Kingdoms, God's Kingdom in Heaven, and Satan's Kingdom here on earth, which has had <u>free will</u> to try and entice mankind to do all manner of evil.

The next example I shall present is the creation of mankind, and the Bible says, (Gen 2:7-8, 22) "And the Lord God formed man of dust of the ground, and breathed into his nostrils the breath of life; and man became a living soul. And the Lord God planted a garden eastward in Eden; and there he put the man whom he had formed. And the rib, which the Lord God had taken from man, made him a woman and brought her onto man. (Gen 3:1-4) "Now the serpent was more sibyl than any beast of the field which the Lord God had made; and he said onto the woman, yea, hath God said, ye shall not eat of every tree of the garden? And the woman said onto the serpent, we may eat of the fruit of the trees of the garden: But, of the fruit of the tree which is in the midst of the garden, God hath said, ye shall not eat of it, neither shall ye touch it, lest ye die. And the serpent said unto the Woman, "Ye shall not surly die: For God doth know that in the day ye eat thereof, then your eyes shall be opened, and ye shall be as gods, knowing good and evil."

God created man and woman (Adam and Eve) in His own image in the Garden of Eden. Where they were to live in peace and harmony with the animals, and they would have everything they needed in order to survive, and man was master over everything there. All that God told them were not to eat of the tree of knowledge, and that He would provide and protect them as long as they obeyed Him on this rule. Now the serpent who was Evil was allowed to come into the Garden of Eden and tempt Eve, Adam's wife, and she ate of the tree of knowledge, and Adam ate of the tree also. Thus they had disobeyed God. When God saw what had happen His caste Adam and Eve out of the Garden of Eden and made Adam worked the land for their food, and Eve was to bare children, which would cause her great pains in doing so. Adam and Eve and every generation thereafter would be cast as sinners for as long as mankind walked the face of this earth, and never to be in God's favor again. He also made the serpent to forever claw on its belly.

God had a number of choices as to how He would deal with this situation, namely:

1. He could not have allowed the serpent into the Garden of Eden.
2. Once the serpent entered the Garden of Even He could have destroyed him.
3. He could have destroyed the serpent and erase the knowledge that Adam and Eve had learned and let them stay in the Garden of Eden.
4. He could put Adam and Eve out of the Garden of Eden and not cast their as sins to past onto all of the time mankind while on this earth.

God chose to put Adam and Eve out of the Garden of Eden, and make them sinners, along with every generation thereafter. He chose not to protect Adam and Eve as he had promise.

The finale example I shall use comes from the King James Bible is The Last Days or called The Judgment Day, for it says, (Rev 20:7-10) " And when the thousand years are expired, Satan shall be loosed out of his prison, and shall go out to deceive the nations which are in the four quarters of the earth, Gog and Ma'gog to gather them together to battle: the number of whom is as the sand of the sea. And they went up on the breadth of the earth, and compassed the camp of the saints about, and the beloved city: and fire came down from God out of heaven, and devoured them. And the devil that deceived them was cast into the lake of fire and brimstone, where the Beast and the false prophet are, and shall be tormented day and night forever and ever."

God will judge all those souls that are evil, and cast into the fires of Hell, and those that are good souls shall live in the Promise Land with His Son, Jesus. God will judge millions upon millions of souls that have lived upon this earth as to rather or not they are to have ever lasting life of happiness and joy, or rather they shall have everlasting pain and suffering for not following God while they were here on this earth.

Even here God has choices He could make when confronting evil:

1. After having made His judgments as to which souls shall have everlasting life of happiness, or have everlasting damnation in the fires of Hell, he could eliminate Evil forever and not have worry about it again.
2. He could allow Evil to live on forever (although in damnation).

He chooser's not to destroy Evil, and let it stay on earth away from Heaven. Thus creating the possibility in the future that Evil shall again be able to have power over human beings if God chooses to allow mankind to live on the earth again, and we would have the same problems that have gone on ever since mankind was created by God, and Evil would be a lasting problem for God.

Thus, in the examples above I have shown different circumstances where God had a chance to eliminate Evil all together, and not allowing Evil to have its way over everything it came in contact with. The first example where the Arch-Angel had turned to Evil, and wanted to take over Heaven, and where Satan tried to eliminate God and take over all power therein; you can clearly see that if God choose to He could have destroy Evil right then, rather than placing Evil elsewhere to grow stronger as time went on, thus forever causing a problem for God any time He tried to create good. Plus, God had not created mankind at this time so the matter of allowing man to have free will was not an option.

In the second example God would have been better served if He had not allowed the serpent into the Garden of Eden, thus allowing Him to tempt Adam and Eve into eating of the tree of knowledge? God really left Adam and Eve with a no win situation, because they knew nothing of Satan, or of Evil, they could not even begin to be able to fight that which they had no knowledge of, and this was the beginning of the fall of mankind. Did not God have the power to warn Adam and Eve of the danger they were in, and did He not promise Adam and Eve His protection from any harm? Surely to punish mankind for the first original sin of which he had no knowledge of seems to me not be of a merciful and loving God.

In the third example where it is the Judgment Day and God separates the good souls from the bad souls, would it not served God to eliminate Evil then, for Evil has no real purpose for existing anymore, except to keep the fires of Hell going for the damnation of the souls Satan has been given control of. You would think in the end of this battle that Satan and God have waged for the souls of mankind that after it was over with God being the victor, God could and should have destroy all forms of Evil forever.

Looking over the examples that I have presented here, and the evidence therein I believe that I have shown that the possibility exist that God cannot eliminate Evil. I say that God and Evil have the same amount of power and one cannot eliminate the other. For if God can also see what is to come in the future then He knew of all that was to happen in regards to mankind and this earth. He knew that Adam and Eve had no chance to win against the serpent in the garden. I cannot believe that God would have allowed all the suffering of children and the human race as a whole, since He says He is a good and merciful God.

It would seem to me that a God who created mankind in His own image would not and could not allow it to suffer just for the sake of free will. I say if God let Evil roam the earth for the sake of letting us have free will to choose good over evil, then I say that He also let Evil have <u>free will</u>; in that after He threw Satan out Heaven did He not give Satan <u>free will</u> over all the earth. This to me means that there is a possibility that God cannot eliminate Evil, for surly if He could He would not have given Satan so much <u>free will</u> and power where God would always battle for the souls of mankind.

Thus, this leads to me believe that there is a possibility that God and Evil have the same amount of power, and most live in this cosmos together forever. Although I cannot based any of what I have presented as fact I feel that I have showed enough evidence that this possibility does exist, and that it is a real possibility that God is not all powerful as we have been lead to believe.